THE PLACE ONE IS

THE PLACE ONE IS

Martha Ronk

OMNIDAWN PUBLISHING
OAKLAND, CALIFORNIA
2022

Cover photograph by Marth Ronk, color modified by Courtney Gregg

Cover typefaces: Helvetica and Garamond Premier Pro
Interior typeface: Garamond Premier Pro

Cover design by Courtney Gregg. Interior design by Ken Keegan

Library of Congress Cataloging-in-Publication Data

Names: Ronk, Martha Clare, author.
Title: The place one is / Martha Clare Ronk.
Description: Oakland, California : Omnidawn Publishing, 2022. | Summary:
    "Martha Ronk's The Place One Is uses excellently selected variations in
    form to reflect on myriad alternatives to the ways we each approach our
    relationship to self, and our relationship to the places in which we sense
    that our being resides. Ronk grounds her poems in the California in
    which she lives, with moving emphases on its variations of landscape, its
    Pacific shoreline, and how much it is challenged by the ecological crises
    of our time. By speaking with courage and candor about the California in
    which she lives, she creates an unforgettable testament that goes beyond
    the particulars of this state, and speaks to all of us wherever we live, now
    and in the future. The Place One Is offers readers a revelatory performance.
    Her language is both immediate, and able to transcend this moment"
    —Provided by publisher.
Identifiers: LCCN 2022006897 | ISBN 9781632431035 (trade paperback)
Subjects: LCGFT: Poetry.
Classification: LCC PS3568.O574 P58 2022 | DDC 811/.54--dc23/
    eng/20220303
LC record available at https://lccn.loc.gov/2022006897

Omnidawn Publishing, Oakland, California
www.omnidawn.com   (510) 237-5472
10 9 8 7 6 5 4 3 2 1
ISBN: 978-1-63243-103-5

I
Each detachable makes up this country I'm pointed into.

A place is a piece of the whole environment that has been claimed by feelings.
A Sense of Place: The Artist and the American Land
—A. Gussow

TO LET GO

imprecise morning as if limbs were only loosely threaded in the coming

and going of tides, in flattened grazing land extending into beach sand

going on until far out of view, the imprint of a foot then another,

the time it takes for a seeded oyster basket to mature

I think of visiting the morning while I am at it, keep saying I am here,

and she writes back from the other coast, we will die where we are,

here or there, hours once rung by bells, she tells me we need to give over

to place-time, the beaches with bleaching logs so many of them,

as if she were telling me something else, I can never not think it means

something hidden from view and wonder then if every detail—

even if distance blurs it—opens to the beating of wings going off

over the flatland and disappearing into migratory patterns,

as if in the near future all objects would simply let go all intensity

TOUCHING

to muse, locate the fringes of steady-on, to put a hand out

to touch solace—the foot of the bed at night inching around it

stepping in wet sand yellow foam washing up the smell of rot,

a girl at the shallow's edge bending to touch it,

a sudden opening under foot where water's worn the concrete jetty

coming to an understanding both of them hope it is so

it is unsure although they continue to touch moving in and out of rooms,

 no putting off the way time manifests age—

painted in the muted colors of accoutrements and darkness

hands folded in that certain way thumbs forming a circle—

at the edge of the myrtles by the water a neglected midden

once you know, it feels like ground one oughtn't step on

ANOTHER WORLD

A walk down Victor Ave to the local park, past the sounds night makes

The use of hiking sticks after a neurological deficit, and misplaced abilities

Misplaced into another world she said, and I wondered how it was she
knew

We know each aspect is weighted, is that the right word for location

Almost everything happens at the liminal

The field is pocked with gopher holes, trees scarred from Frisbee golf

Each stone gets into anyone's shoe, trips and crumbles at any edge

Each person feels differently about trees, the need to plant more trees

If I say I don't like it, it hurts the person who likes it

Each person can distinguish his own sounds, and those of his neighbor

Having fallen backward over the wall, she holds her arm tight in a sling

When's it time to suggest another, hold one's tongue, but for how long

Neighborhoods manage their cars, gossip, windows impolite to look into

ANOTHER COUNTRY

The *it* in *with-it* shifts & pivots as a compass needle

vetch, clover, brackish seaweed in heaped up smells

bits of pulverized shell, skeletal casings underfoot

fog banks stoked by fires in the central valley,

scrims cover what yesterday stood as branched trees, a

house barely visible—more memory than memory,

unheimlich as if and as if it had been or could have been

you whom I turn to in near-sleep stumbling over ourselves,

whose arms and legs was it I thought you called

extracting the changed angle between two norths

a skeleton of rusted car seams laid out on the beach

each step unlinked from the one before

each detachable makes up this country I'm pointed into

Pulled into Earth, Air, Sky

1.

Where One Is

the place one is is the place that is one—nowhere else
and although I can think myself back into some places,
where one is is the only place and everyone's feet
change underfoot as wet, sand, concrete, pebbles and smooth
operate as adjustments or the particular tree out the window
one branch hanging down (o Robert Adams I do think
of your black and white photos but it's a cypress hanging down
outside the window and sending out fingers of that certain green
not the various gray you do so well since one can't be otherwise
than an equation of such enormously specific greens
and one cannot be otherwise than where one is knit into it
beyond windowglass, a fusion with a wind-shaped tree

by 2050 30% of the inhabitable earth may well be desert

2.

IN THE SKY

in the sky would be as others have recognized a highly improbably move,
yet no doubt all humans have dreamed such—just their sounds and cries
call it up—the gliding sideswoop raptors mostly, but in the twilight
the swallows take to the abundant flying insects as if nothing else
had ever existed, and that swarm near the edge of Peninsula road
is one place to be on this peninsula not so different from any others,
these birds no words can get hold of—no adjectives, fonts, metaphors—
how could even an ode praise one of them enough even out of the sky
as an egret lifts one leg then another in slow progress in the shallows,
undulating white against gray (*unda/wave*), language fails bird
moving along as if water were an element to be distained

Leonardo envisioned a device to be built of wood, reeds and taffeta.
"A small model can be made of paper with a spring-like metal shaft that
after having been released, after having been twisted, causes the screw to
spin up into the air."

3.

DREAM WALKING

walking smoothly is a place in the unconscious as one is nightly
with a field laid out in unearthly ochre as far as the eye can see—
it is an occurrence within the frame of lifting out of what we call day
intruding even in the space called night, one needs to keep walking
until such activities are behind, to the side, dismissed as *never mind*,
and get to where one is walking smoothly and without thinking
without effort such as tends to restrict movement before the frame
opens up the yellow-green commons conducive to walking smoothly
without props or artificial aids attaining an easy gait
leaving behind all social hierarchy/ tyranny/ corruption/ greed walking
outside the border of consciousness, all bewilderment gone from a
body only there occurring and not occurring in the same space and for
a time being, the very time within which one is walking

*The commons is a new way to express a very old idea—that some forms of
wealth belong to all of us, and that these community resources must be
actively protected and managed for the good of all.*

4.

F/LIGHT

in the seaweed strewn across the tide line the Least Sandpipers
settle to feed, until suddenly they're off in a great wave
miniscule flecks of light switching on and off, lifting up,
a Mobius strip twisting away into nothing and back again at great speed
until at a spot recognized by some mechanism humans lack
they touch down momentarily before sweeping off again
in a line of white hallucinations you can't keep up with, can't see how
they don't knock one another out of the air given such urgency
and immobile as you are, you're caught up in the blinding cloud
of indistinguishable birds unable to pull away, unable to do anything
but give in as if some *substance* for which you have no name
enabled adherence to the steak of light the flip of their wings releases
at the top line of water like a large fish about to breach the surface

*Hence therefore it comes to pass, that Whiteness is the usual colour of
Light; for Light is a confused aggregate of Rays imbued with all sorts of
Colours, as they are promiscuously darted from the various parts of
luminous bodies.* Isaac Newton

5.

GEOMETRY

the line from your eyes to where they dry themselves strings out
to where cormorants without enough oil in their ragged wings
open them to the elements of air and sun and the line from you
to the cormorants moves across the water to a point
on the undulations of head and neck to the glossy black-blue at the throat,
 connects to a group perched one by one on the wooden poles at the docks
 rhyming themselves into the preening and affected egotism of crows,
marine crow from the Latin—definitely they are there, inserted as points
along a geometry of infinite lines as are you, is where you are:
two lines that meet in a point are called intersecting lines and the line
continues to connect you through your aching midsection to the sea,
definitely the sea into which they go and islands, lagoons,
variegated greenery, sky and space: *a space extending infinitely*
in all directions/you might think of it as the inside of a box (Euclid)

Birds find their way to their destination thanks to their ability to sense
the Earth's magnetic field. Its lines create an angle with the surface of the
Earth, except at the equator. The angle and field intensity is sensed by
birds, thanks to a type of protein located in their eyes called
'cryptochromes'. Therefore, their eyes work like a magnetic compass that
guides them during their journeys. zooportraits.com

Re-claiming Reclamation

irony inserts itself in cattle grazing on "reclaimed" wetlands

one sly remark after another they just calm me down looking at them

driving route 255 through mounds of cloud before burn off

the barns a zigzag of roof like sharp creases of paper

and it never, almost never snows here but I can't stop seeing sheets of it

sliding off in winter, off that crisp weathered fold

lands reclaimed from lagoons and marshland drained 1890 (90%)

for crops, cattle, marshes and wetlands named in documents a *hindrance*

a word used for water, fish, birds, insects, frogs, and dragonflies

their small engines propelled by glassy wings of starchy chitin

and an architecture of veins close to my shoulder

a green see-through sheen over *The End of Days*, Jenny Erpenbeck

and it does seem the end is so close, two sets gliding and cutting through air

near whatever waters and since before the dinosaur

but irony comes round again: reclaimed lands reclaimed for sloughs, lagoons for all the hindrances including humans with binoculars turned

on a black and white bird the guide says perhaps a night heron

hunkered over

6500 acres of fresh and salt water marshland existed on Humboldt Bay in the 1800s. Now there is less than 1/10 of that and only 40 acres of freshwater marsh (Arcata's Marsh Project now almost doubles the amount of freshwater marsh on Humboldt Bay). Salt marshes store enormous quantities of carbon, essential to plant productivity, by, in essence, breathing in the atmospheric carbon and then using it to grow, flourish and increase the height of the soil. Even as the grasses die, the carbon remains trapped in the sediment. The researchers' model predicts that under faster sea-level rise rates, salt marshes could bury up to four times as much carbon as they do now.

BROKEN BIRDS

A crack in the edifice, an ivy sprawl through the wall, a damp coming at
you and spill

                                    sleeky slicks on the water,
                      feathers

encrusted with the stuff and the poor things wizened and wet.

                           We won't talk of it we say

and then begin, headaches moving off the coast and the beaten back frailties

coming on strong.

                    Blackened, tarred,

oozing through the oil, eating *polyaromatic hydrocarbin*

                       feathers in a sodden mess,

beaky ruination of flight, that unspooled skim across the waters,

                        pulled down by a spill, a crack in the Halliburton,

the leaks we tend not to talk about.

*The **spill** poses particular risks to brown **pelicans**. If the birds dive into **oil**-slicked waters while foraging, their feathers could become saturated, causing them to suffer from hypothermia or even drown. Audubon*

MIDDENS

garbage heap in Scandinavian, *mykdyngia* (manure pile): midden,

left-overs, detritus—bits of fishbone, mortars, elkhorn wedges,

obsidian knives broken to free the spirit, bone spears, skeletons,

decaying trees dug from Gunther's well on Indian Island

> *and from what I can see from the corner of the window*
> *and under the endangered myrtles at the water's edge*
> *white bits of clamshells scattered about in the dirt*
> *broken, strewn, one of many mounds left by Wiyots 900-1860*

so many on Indian Island as to lift the elevation as they paddled dug-outs

into eelgrass and rushes at low enough tide to slide in among the weeds

handpick clams out of the shallows and toss shells in the air

> *my hand moving over the corrugated shell ridge*
> *clogged with dirt how long have they been at the edge I can't think,*
> *never sat so close to a people so violently slaughtered*

after he bought Tuluwat Island it was renamed Gunther Island,

then vigilantes killed 80 to 250 Wiyots with axes, knives, guns—

one woman, it was said, survived by hiding in a trash heap

whose scavenged past do we walk on, what do we leave,
tossed out at the Eureka dump a bin for corrugated cardboard, one
for hard plastic, bottles in the bin for shattering glass

called a stone age people the Wiyots left no pottery shards

but shells of excreted calcium carbonate layer over layer

and interwoven baskets of upright hazel sticks,

willows, conifer roots, bear grass, dyed porcupine quills,

taking women a year or more, black triangles, lightning bolts

Scraps of indigenous history

scratched hinterlands and the farflung   cased behind glass,

collected in multiples   piecemeal and over time

stitched with fishing twine   housed in museum vaults

the ongoing   catapulted into waters moving out to

unfinished sentences   songs of smoke   marks on clay

a leg lifted in a dance   no one remembers

land lived on is only for feet   dusty imprints blown away

a headdress   woven   feathered   ribbon-trimmed

beauty seared into skin   tattooed stripes on the chin

scraps of uninformed information   eluded, erased

land forms   left snake-like   telling us in what dialect

anonymous was what   was Wiyot   was imprinted with a map

was dark of face   was blue unborn   was landlocked

was unnamed   was pictured only as the unseen

PLACED, MISPLACED

to be in a place is to be placed, and for most means the familiar,

people in what *is* as it is thought to be, meaning weather, meaning
   seagreen,

meaning *it was an osprey* naming it by name, or a Buckeye, a highrise,

the Allegheny under copper green bridges, going over in snowdrifts,
   smells

of lime, sauerkraut, sweat—to be a body changes place itself, impinges

into the closer, blurrier, not-for-me, displaced and without shoes,
   without

doorway or song, having been wrenched away—

no longer a pint or two, no common tongue, no dead stones

*the loss of what's needful: c.1200, niedfulle, "necessary, needed, useful,"
also "in want, poor, hungry, starving, having or exhibiting need or
distress," from need (n.) + ful. Meaning "characterized by need" is from
mid-13c. From mid-14c. as "indispensable, necessary," also "urgent,
demanding attention."*

THE EDGES

She says we'll see it if we walk up high enough but that was last week
and the Great Blue was gone before the top of the rise where the sky
would be Bay but for the black stripe, eyes making out only a fine line
anchoring itself, although this morning even it is missing and I see
that coming to know colors, shapes, minute particulars of the wetlands
(as with the desert it took me so long to see) takes time and now it all
comes full at me at the edges—reeds, rushes, sedges, hodgepodge tilted
and crosshatched, bent and upright stuff strangling along fences
and highways—dandelions, plastic cups, weedy, tossed-aside,
ever-present Queen Anne's lace from off-white to curled-in-on-itself,
persistent, bristly—shape-shifting on its thin stem, paper cut-out,
cauliflower, mythic and edible, one drop of blood, the thin backbone
of a county, no hyperbole, just the unseen ordinary where the road's
painted with *schoo xing* where there's no school, no school bus.

Illusions of Motive

Illusions of motive as fog colors itself gray, white,
bullnosed, then fragmented fingerclouds passing Trinidad's rock
we call this darkening beforehand, evening,
the purposeful seemingly located in the moving of
imperceptible air,
                        the mélange of so-called
motives for what seem motiveless shifts, desiccation relocating
entire herds, fiery grass exploding, filaments of mind set adrift,
chemical intrusions into synapse, obsessions over cryptocurrency,
conspiracies, the everlasting dying of a species

fog slides soundlessly onto mudflats, a glaze slipping across
        would-be water
effortless seedwings in adjacent fields, underfoot and earthborn
branches overhead splitting and moving darkly upward.

No place

no place unfraught no easy slide into a tepid sea

no place tenderhearted and thoroughly fertile

no place transpires as night intensifies

no place picked up and left high and dry

no place downpour from the porch lightning highlights

no place I didn't love you or over time moved the iron bed

no place Joshua Trees and Oaks and willows and weeping

no place auras, tents in flyaway gullies

no place rusty moldy soaked on alternate Fridays

no place too hot too dim and too many words for snow

no place I haven't been anywhere much less often

no place insouciance I figured how costly it might be

no place that year I moved angles around and took up arms

no place a sea of troubles, the sea itself rising and rising

WHAT NEXT

what might turn into what   grow out of mud into what

what place might humans have   in the aftermath

so awkwardly creaturely   lumpish with legs

switching language around   as if it could save us

on the phone she says   moldy bread was put on wounds

civil war wounds or mushrooms or dirt—

there's garbage in the Balboa creek watershed   chip bags

Styrofoam clams   plastic this's and that's congealing

someday   computer-altered frog cells will eat them

yet the present   undoes us

damns our creaturely minds   self-destructive with intent

crows must have been something else before   so self-assured

skies marked up with ink pens   they roll around on ant hills

pick locked boxes   laugh at us clumsy sorts

even ground water doesn't last   we once imagined

oceans swirling   unending   water into water

A PLACE THAT ONCE WAS

the postcard of Chinatown the sole remnant
of the place and those who worked the rails
who collected for a time in Eureka
collected blue and white rice bowls
collected hats worn in time-worn photographs
cleared the land, forged and set the rails,
hung over chasms in baskets to set explosives
who were paid $26 a month
for families, back in Canton Province
15,000 came 600 died working
and when bosses set up competition
along ethnic or racial lines
the Chinese won hands down
and when a man was killed by a stray bullet at 4th and E
were broken into groups and driven out
the area a powder keg by then
Asians scarce in the place today

Courtesy of Barbara Voss
Bamboo-pattern rice bowls were found near a railroad tunnel
camp site near Donner Lake.
On display at Old Jail Museum, Truckee-Donner Historical Society.

Piecemeal, we're all

reddish buckwheat lies low, slippage in each step

the s-curve of the Blue's neck straightens and swallows

seafoam a random pattern of dissolution

the distance moving further down in early fog

a small figure turns out not to be nor is smoke smoke

a thick brushmark in the upper corner slumps over

strands of seaweed grow longer as time slithers its wet

pinkish skeletons inch up from below

bits unhinged from other bits against a preparatory wash

the juncture of hip to limb, muscle to joint

what you are is not so different from what you see,

all's piecemeal, Middle English *pece* (piece) + *mele* (at a time)

From Middle English pecemele, from pece ("piece") + mele (from Old English mælum ("at a time"), dative plural form of mæl ("time, measure")), taking the place of Old English styccemælum ("in pieces, bit by bit, piecemeal; to pieces, to bits; here and there, in different places; little by little, by degrees, gradually"); equivalent to piece + -meal.

Ma-Lei'l Trail, Arcata California

There are no trees on the beach it goes on and the water's so cold
no one swims and on Ma-Lei'l the trees are being swamped
by giant dunes migrating over them as wind blows grains of sand
into the air and they hang there until they're over the top and falling
on ragged limbs and ragged tree hair (*Itla-okla*) smothering the tree
until each tree kneels into the sand and over the years
the slump of the dunes alters the landscape—
the movingness of the world is right with us on this trail
moving country into country, one history wiping out another,
upending a familiar world shifting and moving over cities,
lives, shoulders too weighted down to think with, no matter
how little or much one knows—shifting sand moves over trees,
fills up ponds and lagoons, chokes a night with images
of future migrations extending into where we are walking.

*When enough grains are gathered, gravity <u>results in small sand-slides</u>
<u>downward</u>. Thus the leeward slope of a dune is often referred to as the
"slipface."* livescience.com

*A Wiyot tribal name, the property comprises wetland and associated
uplands including dunes and maritime forest within a barrier island
ecosystem and includes habitat for the endangered Menzies Wallflower,
and beach Layia, as well as the rare dune mat plant community.*

**Native Americans told them the plant was called *Itla- okla*,
which meant "tree hair."**

Solitary

solitary is a category powerful as gender, but not gender

as place orchestrates a body equal to its own windswept

uninhabited landforms I walk no matter the weather,

the same route inching past other shapes indecipherable

one from the other—bulky, sturdy, hunched,

all signs of identity, vacated, all us newly swathed creatures,

as in the fogged distance a domed head, solitary comrade,

featureless and pressing hard into ocean wind

as the sole upright on the flattened beach comes slowly

into view but never moving into a category other than

ineluctably private, unrecognizable, solo

Into rising waters

under the various moons, various translations thereof

so many vacant lots, Matilija poppies, trash and abandonment,

thistles, rusty blackberries, coyote brush, tires, see-through pale flax,

clumps of fog heave back and forth as if they were mammalian

labial creatures pulsing earthward then into cloudshorn skies

each iteration a different tidal moon torn into papery scraps

refracted light burns my eyes, a cramped muscle turns the street lamp blue

under the rubbery step the gravel gives way

restless wheat stalks akin to what muttering is like

under her breath, in another room talking to herself,

thin and highpitched, underpinning whole fields of words,

a lens of fresh water floats on the heavier salt water under that—

if you push the weeds a marker stands where the winter tide was high—

rising seawater will swamp a nearby town, the bridge, the Mad River slough

the low-lying field where the cows lie and stand, the graffiti-covered barn

REFLECTION

Reflection takes over trees more in than out and mirrors the question

of how similar underwater branches are to those up against the sky

independently placed and yet decidedly one blurred entity,

and yet how differently the reflection moves under cover of duck weed

under the rush of wind-water as it shoves green islands from arc to arc

on the rounded pond, or skidding across diameters—breaks the union,

unhinges leaf from branch and pulls it into water

where it floats until it no longer does, as leaves in autumn fall and flatten

into dull shards, remnants of green, forward and back in time

taking place over and under water as we make our way around the pond

and make ourselves by increments in the time and trees it takes,

unknowingly, one foot in front of the other, shoes muddy and damp.

*I perceive that more or other things are seen in the reflection than in the
substance.* —Journal, 9 December 1856 Thoreau

Predictions of finitude

running headlong into nothing is nothing like the optical illusion

    of its blank stare

could mirror back the entire day you were walking and the history

    of northern California

weather patterns which tell more about the way anyone feels about anything

    than even the spume

of oracle flashing up on the beach you can see over the horizon

    or is it under, well in any case

after a while who can stand the predictions of finitude which even

    the infinite fog conveys

Dementia Elegy

Entire landscapes, weathermaps missing these years you're gone,

I mistakenly read a *mistrial* of rain, how it rained in the woods,

cold-pierced, rhododendron-dripping, whole sections of books

wiped out like half a brain as talk neglects words you never did

if only I could say it to you missing bright sun on the daylilies

lined up on my walk to you, you don't know of it, the whole place

a ruin, and so much you knew about now found nowhere—

ash at the base of fruit trees and the names of plants in Latin,

words we both needed to root us, a need to plead misery

remembering that huddle on the floor of the car dusty with self

is everywhere, must always have been, but the brain slows

no way you could imagine what it is reading a letter you wrote.

LEAVING IS ALSO A PLACE

Leaving moves into us, taking us from this place

where we are and from the place we're going

into some third bi-furcated in-between

as a swollen door doesn't quite close,

no furniture floats about the rooms

but all groundings are weakened

tattered bird wings droop from the poles

and leaving has a look and smell of its own, guano, snow

in the wrong season and the geese passing

aren't migrating but stopping to feed in cow pastures,

we must do it each in the ways we are,

changing definitions of *obliged, of memorable,*

each set of wings, each threatening storm,

movement slivers the floorboards

and leaving's geographical

Night: a photograph by Robert Adams

Ordinary bits of light on neighborhood leaves, trees passed by,

spattered not-very-white on a random number of them,

the canopy of leaves wide enough to hold multiple bits of light

and what I can't help is how pulled I am into the lights as if my eyes

could focus on multiple places at once which I know they can't

and yet my body, flattened and splayed, spreads itself over the leaves

and the branch never lowers or moves, simply stays as it is

as I am pulled from each limb and finger, head and elbow onto the tree

as if I could just lie there elongating out to the extreme endpoints

not in my neighborhood but in his Longmont neighborhood in 1976

when at that time I was nowhere near and yet the on-line

allows me to move entirely into a night and lights

scattered I suppose from an ordinary street lamp on the sidewalk

and the tree branches and it must be summer given so many leaves.

NIGHT TREES

each tree sticks itself upward dark into light or light's the medium

for each to define itself aslant against air saturated with water

pixelated molecules diffusing the already diffused source of light

so few here, so few houses, few on the street, the homeless cyclist

crossed noises crossing the highway, uneasiness tossed

in empty bottles off to the side, infirm gullies underfoot

past the corner sudden quiet, sudden removal from all else

and then there's each tree, its leafless sticks, some quiver in haze

some gather themselves, rising up into Japanese brooms

(an inventory of the tightly bound, stiff and ancient)

and there they are, numerous V's in and above, and one's own upright

seemingly held, in lower-down lost-in the-dark conjunction.

THE HALLUCINATED PLACE OF NIGHT

In a slurry of dark and light, night picks out light not the other way
around—the curvy shadow of branches, the reflective shine, the lull
between stem and stem,

leaking into black sorrel undergrowth and with the passing of centuries
extra trunks on redwoods fuse and flow together and branches move
horizontally, bridges from trunk to trunk from limb to limb, and it is
dark,

no way to visualize a dark that can't be seen, memory leeching away,
dark undercurrents of connections one to another across thresholds,
and in the center

how black-suited, how back-turned they all appear late as it is and strange,
night enclosing and opening, as dimly this face and that one slide through

fusing with us as we make our way stumbling over uneven paving into
another time as the interstices of the brain weaken and allow for seepage

we tend to huddle and branch, shedding outer garments as trees shed bark
dropping woolens and jackets in tandem as if agreed upon

the surreal occurring more frequently as I'm near the black trees
reaching into further dissolve, nightly disfiguration.

II
Familiar/Unfamiliar

Fear no more the heat o'th' sun
Nor the furious winter's rages;
Thou thy worldly task hast done,
Home art gone and ta'en thy wages.
Golden lads and girls all must,
As chimney-sweepers, come to dust.

MELANCHOLY OF SUNLIGHT

Melancholy of sunlight grips the sidewalk and shines back at those few

slipping by, shutting their eyes tight against its flannelly familiarity,

crossed arms keeping it all in and for what, given the uncontrollable winds,

friction in the ribs, anything other than this ache of bright,

this center of the universe wildly scattered about the sky—its ascendance

worse than lack and loss and then the frantic flight of birds up into it,

black and dusky their wings, distances from one spot to another so vast

and lacking all foresight they flap their way into the blinding light.

RUINOUS LIGHT

Ruin and ruinous light and one's eyes.

Nothing between. Nothing shadows. Nothing supposed.

Less likely than superficial, less qualified than aluminum.

One window in the side of. One stucco. One all-over light.

Too many skins out for no mercy,

no shadowy abrupt, just flat forever and ever.

Intervenes another skin in blue where the woman next door

is watching out the rear window is herself turned on for hours.

One rectangle of fluorescence no interruption, no speaking back

only the monotone that blinds our eyes

in the syrupy light pouring over everything.

IN THE TWILIGHT

In the twilight of twins there are identical pictures on either side.

Someone from next door is blaring the way it was.

Shapes in musical form.

Each one gets a lamp and the orange triangle of an abstract.

Each house's a match. Each roof. Each grazing land with weeds.

It's meant to be holy, no one would choose it otherwise:

the legs of a woman hanging up a sheet to dry, a man coiling a hose.

> *For all flesh is as grass, and all the glory of man as the flower of*
> *grass. The grass withereth, and the flower thereof falleth away.*

Dishevelment takes up so much room, everyone displaced and highwire.

In the heat there's nowhere to drive to despite the invitation to.

You wish for the shadow of sound, squint into the sunshine,

say, say a little prayer for me.

THE BLUE HOUR

so blue it cancels itself   darkening into itself   was it
what night   thrusting myself into it   as a stroke of charcoal
saying Tuesday's   ordinary as paper and went to
where love   was brick and its evocative tendencies
whose wrist and its twisting   its particular twisting
how to make a mark I asked about   how to do it
the paper sits flat   I couldn't hear at that distance
a book stood between   night and how we talked of it
blue sleeves shortened into wrists   night coming on
in the brick building   a hallway and maroon carpet
could have been   then wasn't   a moon, a hall light
you leap onto the paper   it darkens with several marks
each apartment you've ever   a love on the other side
could I learn it   like living it again on paper
touching   charcoal night   blue pressed rag

THE SOUND OF COYOTES IN THE CANYONS

Each time she chooses to be wily, her silence undoes.

So there's always something.

So and So, a common name.

At table she said, then he said, and then it was over.

Out there a sound of coyotes and falling things.

Nothing in the option or screenplay is finished for good.

We designed a rhetoric even when we wanted something else.

Getting up to get something isn't like that.

Polarized into positions even in silence.

The film she showed me was about things falling,

she had taken it from another movie and added sound

to the things falling down on the TV and in the other room.

When it broke into shards we thought of it as archeological not personal.

> *The failed operatic of coyotes scrambling for a spot on the stage*
> *of sky so far away the hens cry murder in their sleep. Their turn*
> *will come at dawn, noises projected across fields to those still*
> *finding their seats.*

LA FISSURES

the sidewalk I walk on is cracked
      in the fissure   there's azure blue pale at the edges,

behind the eyelids, faces   morphing, lines of ink
stringing themselves
                there's the nursery on York,

The York Nursery, a field of dust, empty   the façade blanched
\in the sun-scalding streets with body shops and the *York Bar*

abrupt marks in the thinking I am watching
                      seeing it skip

as LP's skipped,   a blanking out,   blurred faces
                tracking a history I don't want to track

the sidewalk lifts and cracks   I see her tape up
paintings to protect colors, peel it off

all the Japanese nurseries vacant on Hyperion
closed iron gates,
                once a glimpse of pale flowers
her pale powder

            painting faces Goya almost

made them of darkness & tar   *unidentified* shows up on

the phone window
superfluous the only answer

THE IMPRINT OF THE ORDINARY

The imprint of the ordinary happens each day by
the oak trees.

If you know they are there.

In the city he argues with a friend you both know.
They sit in an office and shift their chairs.

The secret influence of stars, the conceit of this imperfect stay.

Oak trees form an arch and the difference is noticeable in each of us.
It isn't only the pleasure of the moment I have to believe.

We walk down by the creek and come back muddied and wet.

If the stars are where you know they are.
If you could figure out even why you wanted it.

O shut the door and when thou has done so come weep with me.

The oaks are growing moss on the north side.
On the green leaves of the thistle there's a spill of white.

In the city the argument comes and goes.
They turn their eyes away and look at the postcard on the wall.

The oak trees drape over one another, covered in Spanish moss.
He takes it off the wall and hands it over.

OUR BODIES IN THE SCATTERED LIGHT

If we think with our bodies moving around in the scattered light
it can't be fixed without destroying the scattered light.
How could one build a form of what's been through the years.
And what he wants is history sitting at the table with him
all the years and all of us who've been there
no matter he can't forgive any of us for what we've done.
I'm afraid I can't return his call.
The one sitting next to me is the one I want to talk to
what if I don't know a thing about him
leaving history behind in a sealed room or trying to think of the coffee
one has already still sleeping in his bed.
And the machine keeps recording messages
from days before as if voices were hanging in the air.
There in the cubicle where he was expected
where the light through the slats is as vivid as history.
This approximation of a life is what is drying on the side of a hill
and has a name I can fix only in an approximation of words.
What I want to say is I want to have been your past even if you could
never forgive me for it before we met.

What it's not

The strange was merely that off-kilter strange
yet even the smallest these days seems to require
readjustments in temperament.
Last night my last thought was I must look it up
as soon as it's light, but haven't I gone through it now
with no recollection of what in this edition isn't there.
I think of all who are missing in this life
and when someone occurs to me it's like being pulled
in the two directions I'm pulled in at night.
You say it's not the ferocity of those crows,
not the reviews or terrifying news of the day.
You say it's not the music—so very loud—
and definitely, *no more eloquence.*
The moon calms down in the moist night air.
I remember his saying something about the second to the last line.
What can it mean if you can only love someone
if you *abide by the unspoken agreement not to say so.*
There are, he says to me, on leaving,
many things you've already decided not to say.

RECOGNIZING ONESELF

The body is no longer what it was, more an along-the-highway sort of thing

each part struggling to keep up with other struggling bits and limb forms

in the dream I am bagging up leaves and sticks blown in by a mighty wind

in every corner of the weathered barn, dragging sweeping sweating,

yet the master shows only the back of a raincoat and refuses our efforts

on his behalf, was it my kung fu master who had us kicking the air

on a floor waxed with dancer's wax, was it Sifu now dead himself

who said I could keep the quilt if I liked, old and dirty as it was,

wrap yourself up at night he said, how often the dream is bagging up

against a leaking present, endless sweeping not as leading to anything

but a useless effort in a structure near collapse and in need of repair

as the apartment where I sanded the floors and painted them deck-white

as if and always as if, but these days I wouldn't do it, would break

the silence, wouldn't recognize myself any more than I already do.

Vocabularies of fire

Smoke and fire enter vocabularies of breathing,

constricted, airways, asthmatic, particulates,

the upturned belly of a frog through dimmed eyes
        turns out suddenly a leaf

compromised trees in a drought-state,

lungs weakened by second-hand smoke

each breath a rasp

        a leaf changes definition, becoming *fuel*

throughout the basin claustrophobia's closing in

        the cloister keeps us *clauster/cloister*

and grammar encloses us in shallow intakes,

packable documents, meds, albums,

rashes (combined in equal parts with misery)

stamp a fire tattoo up the right arm

        a leaf's fingers curl up, combust in the heat

birds restless in sunlight too brilliantly bright,

droning a high-pitched operatic

(in the 70's Didion wrote of birds exploding in air).

The bird population in North America has dropped by three billion—or 29 percent—since 1970, and a warming planet is changing the migration patterns of many bird species, according to a 2019 study published in Science.

,

Paranoia LA

Some drag-along solipsistic's turned up the noise again,

and getting some sleep's a difficult slow-me-down

given the overdone and misplaced attention to one's every move,

the smallest noise and itch and then the mind's off and running.

It's unavoidable these days and altogether thrivable in a city

with its swiveling of necks as if someone's following

or angle-wise, either of which might stand as a rescue,

serve as stand-in for an optimal solution to whatever,

easier to clothe suspicion in its hooded fang,

to hear the slithers crawl than to calm the red seas,

stop the tell-tale heart, whatever's beating behind the wall.

THE HOMELESS: A DRIVE-BY

1.
Roots of trees and random sticks—a crawlspace
scattered with what light makes its way into the tangles of
where hidden-from-view had slept and left
an empty Budweiser, the ovals of eucalyptus,
newspaper standing in for floorboards, bits of tonal sepia

three windows cut in cardboard to mimic a house,
a décor of impossible cold under an LA sky
one towel   one running shoe an aqua
tube of the unreadable in the homeless rooms carved from undersides

passable by   passable by

pretense to be behind closed doors, pretense to be hidden away
in the drive-by onto the freeway
                                        as in an enclosure of time
to where it speeds ahead not to see the already seen.

2.
Indentations in an empty bed roll, the shadow of a week
curled up in the folds of bushes under the freeway
leaves scattered on top.
                              The cup hides its innards,
a coat shifts its arms, its underarms, its wide label
and remnants find their places at right angles to a bottle
rolled down to meet them, plastic fork, empty take-out box,

a single shoe—encampments abandoned to newsprint,
crumpled pornography and a litter of underwear
out of which men have walked into a city unknown.

Location LA

1.
Never arriving in a city missing its location
fixity lost to fermentation not to mention slipping
ground and the onslaught of billboards
and other signposts pointing to someplace certain to have
moved its drywalls further east/west wherever
population shifts have planted their shallow roots.
Eucalyptus brought down by sheer size.
Hotels razed by funding forces.
Gentrification serving up exquisite sandwiches
on tiny tables and planned obsolescence
stands at the ready, ready or not.

2.
Never arriving in a city missing in locational drift
plates shifting under facades and whipped décor,
seas rising and falling at the edge of amusements
and surf. The migrations migrating elsewhere,
monarchs lost on their way south, children coming north
in droves on their way to anywhere else.
The city of lost souls blowing in the winds
and those who are named *not us* no matter who we are.
Where is she now, he asks, whatever happened to the one
named for a saint, the one with the ankle tattoo
the one who got lost, lost out, had only just arrived.

Familiar/unfamiliar

A city noted for its horizontality largely inaccessible without a car,
the inability to climb aboard, the loss of one kind of mobility
substituted by the command: walk, walk.   Baudrillard

It's right out there and yet it escapes me this city I ought to live in,
I do live in and when the morning comes I walk wherever it takes me
in the circle that is my street and the circle around that
and I take this walk with variations associated with the hour
and my so-called ability as one part won't work as it used to work
and the so-called hill once a regular part is no longer included
as it was in some earlier walks of my walking to know where I live,
what plants and birds, what dogs have disappeared into 8x11 signs
on telephone poles or how the jogging, swinging, climbing parts
of what's done continue in ways both routine and arcane
as taking it all in becomes a failed practice, as elusive as what walking is
or might be now to a life in which one never thought about it,
now one always thinks about it all the time in this new stage
in which it is good for you, no longer getting from here to there
or just out for a walk but something different from what it once was
and whatever I finally think about walking I do think that it makes
the familiar unfamiliar and more and more like the city I live in.

On Detective Novels:

*"these were tales characterized by speed of a particularly Angeleno strain.
It was the boom sound, the race of get-rich-quick, of get-'em-before-they-
get-you. "[The novel of speed] tends to be short, and to be marked by
striking economies of style. It leaves little room for the direct expression of
emotion, preferring fascinating surfaces to mere depth. And it is a kind
of novel that seems to arise from, and to be especially suited to, the place
called Los Angeles," where haste is always a question of life or death, and
contemplation, or any consideration of the past, is intolerable." David Wyatt*

The Lady in the Lake

> *"This is the ultimate end of the fog belt, and the beginning of that
> semi-desert region where the sun is as light and dry as old sherry
> in the morning, as hot as a blast furnace at noon, and drops like an
> angry brick at nightfall." (south of San Dimas down into Pomona)*

Heat and its offspring, bright little dots before fainting,
mini-blasts of the furnace-like sun,

the world born in paragraphs before the next crime, before he saunters,
takes off a coat slowly, deliberately

as pages turn slowly as causality
one's fingers complicit, the feel of pulp paper

dipping in and getting off scot free without having rumpled the bedsheets,

while beleaguered Marlowe drives in town and out, up elevators and down
    scuffling, filling the tank, sleuthing the missing wives
    whose mistaken identities fool everyone for a time

one in a red dress, one slinky without ever zipping a zip (those days when
    you had to have a man to do it) one at the bottom
    of the lake

while our hero, slugged from behind, is out cold. . .
    someday it will all come back to you and you won't like it

while we, voyeurs following from a readers' perch,
    like the others not quite right in the head,
    suffer but minor headaches, erratic sleep,
    short snorts.

What did it matter where you lay once you were dead? In a dirty sump or in a marble tower on top of a high hill? You were dead, you were sleeping the big sleep, you were not bothered by things like that. Raymond Chandler

THE BIG SLEEP #1

Marlowe gets up and walks around the orchids and mops his brow,

his underarms are damp.

Chandler inserts obvious metaphors, they unseat the scene.

A few locks of dry white hair clung to his scalp, like wild flowers

> *fighting for life on a bare rock.*

Having nothing to do with the case.

Faces erased into objects wearing creased trousers and pencil skirts.

You can't think in a poem or case like that.

If orchids have the fleshy skin of old men what can you do,

but fill in the blanks or take the bottle of rye out of your back pocket.

I can see it as if in a photograph, arranged to droop or take on a sheen

as if it'd been around awhile. Arranged the operative word.

THE BIG SLEEP #2

*The blue carpet darkened a shade or two and the walls drew back
into remoteness. The chairs filled with shadowy loungers. In the corners
were memories like cobwebs.*

Expanse of blue carpet scuffed up a dusty whiff of it
from the still air of the street to the still air of a complex
where anyone's been before,

                     the entryway to a hunch.

Architecture's the map of mystery, the uncertainty of an elevator,
its momentary glitch. Somewhere beyond the door is somewhere
to get to.

                   Stalled, the first paragraph of a chapter
describes the foyer, the furniture and some insufferable emptiness—
the weight of the unplotted,

                   the material stuff of ironic surprise.

            *Inside, in the square barren lobby, a man put a green
            evening paper down beside a potted palm and flicked a
            cigarette butt into the tub the palm grew in.*

The startle not of blackmail, but of the *green* evening news. Since when.
Another mystery, another time.

Murder's in the details.

THE BIG SLEEP #3

This was another day and the sun was shining again.

No wonder we're cooped inside—Santa Ana's in the driver's seat,
down the dingy side streets empty of shadows to slide into.

Later, as if on the lam, zigzagging from tree top shade to tree top shade
sidestepping the direct glare can't help a mirrored return to:

eyes as windows to the soul, so the guy said, tracking her disappearing heels.

For him too a couple of Scotches. For him too, useless swallows.
The need for a weather-shift to settle settlements.
Like cement-shoes one's innards.
General Sternwood formed by *an economical smile, a wooden gaze.*

It's said identification with character is jejune, but who's it then looking
back
          from a mirror over the bathroom sink, rubbing a chin.

                    There was no sensation in my head.
             The bright glare got brighter.
There was nothing but hard aching white light. Multiple reflections.
    Unshaven.

THE BIG SLEEP #4

*A moon half gone from the full glowed through a ring of mist among
the high branches of the eucalyptus trees on Laverne Terrace. A
radio sounded loudly from a house low down the hill. The boy swung
the car over to the box hedge in front of Geiger's house, killed the
motor and sat looking straight before him with both hands on the wheel.*

Reading the introductory paragraphs more often I walk the streets,
their clothes a blur of suits and wing tips, never did I see anyone so natty
so baggy and shined, almost familiar from a distance
as the fog of orientation overtakes, and bored besides rolls the window,
rolls a joint, only once between finger and thumb,
though it could've been a mimicking gesture as the ultimate of panache,
 but it's the lost time I'm speaking of, the ways the past overlaps
and explains any number of movies in black and white
or when the familiar stroll takes you past a tiny dog attached to a woman
in shorts and wrist weights and you know you're back somewhere
with a moon and mist, the name of the street as sweet as she was,
as when a book opens and the description's as delicious as the plot.

THE BIG SLEEP #5

Description's never the point given the gun to come. Can't hold up its
end of the bargain. Still, it's perpetuity, not causality that counts, holds
up after plots are long gone.
                                        Sticks around after Silver-Wig's
never seen again, her kisses followed by, *You son of a bitch*.

The name's still La Brea, the eucalyptus still fringes the rutted road and
the dust layers our overbuilt and guilty pleasures.

Parking lots turn over in their graves.

Night comes down as hard.

And the moon holds us in its grip, makes the windows what they are
                                        when it's dark and we
all go there.

We take in its bright shape as he offers it up, fitted to the ruinous city
we know and mind somewhat less that nothing so far has happened.

   A moon half gone from the full glowed through a ring of mist
among the high branches of the eucalyptus trees on Laverne Terrace.

Notes

"Melancholy of sunlight," the quotation is from *Cymbeline* 4.2
"In the twilight," King James Bible, Peter 1:24
The Baudrillard quotation is from *Rethinking Architecture*
"Location LA" was influenced by *Paris Spleen*
"Night Trees," the uneven paving stones are from Proust

"Middens": EtpidoL wotperoL contains an extensive shell midden associated with a large precontact and historic Wiyot village. The site figures prominently in Wiyot mythology, had a level flat used for dancing, and its geographic position at the center of the island makes this site highly significant. Among the mythological events at EtpidoL wotperoL is the story of a "medicine-man ...who was the first man of one of the nations," and who sought power from the pelicans flying overhead and obtained strong fishing luck. This attracted many people to live at EtpidoL wotperL. The historic period at the site includes the archaeological remains of the house and agricultural operation of Fredrick Robert Gunther, a German immigrant who purchased the property in 1860 from Captain John T. Moore, the first American to claim Indian Island in 1858. EtpidoL wotperoL is eligible to the National Register of Historic Places. https://insider.si.edu/wp-content/uploads/2016/05/3.jpg

ACKNOWLEDGMENTS

Many thanks to Omnidawn Publishing, to Rusty Morrison and Ken
    Keegan
"Scraps of Indigenous History," is indebted to the work of Ken
    Gonzales-Day
"Dream Walking" for David and Joann James
"The Edges" for Nancy Ihara
"Another World" for Dale Wright
"to let go" for Fanny Howe
"Elegy" in memory of Wayne Winterrowd and Joe Eck, North Hill, VT
"LA Fissures" for Linda Besemer

I am grateful to the editors of the published poems, some revised here.
Many poems in part 2 appeared in a chapbook, "Familiar/Unfamiliar,"
    Magra Books 2016, many thanks to the editor, Paul Vangelisti
"The blue hours," "Recognizing Oneself," "Illusions of Motive,"
    Conjunctions 72 2019
"Another Country, "to let go," "fissures," *Chicago Review* 63/64,
    summer 2021
"Mai'lei," "No place," *Poetry Northwest,* summer/fall 2020
"In the sky," "f/light," "The place of night," "Night (Robert Adams),"
    The Big Other, 2.9.2020
"Night Trees," *Harper's Magazine* July 2020
"into rising waters," *Critical Quarterly*, 8.24.2020

Martha Ronk is the author of twelve books of poetry and one of short stories, *Glass Grapes.* Her poetry books include *Silences* (Omnidawn 2019), *Ocular Proof* (Omnidawn, 2016, on photography), *Transfer of Qualities* (Omnidawn 2013, long-listed for the National Book Award), *Vertigo* (Coffee House Press, a National Poetry Series Selection 2007), *Partially Kept* (Nightboat), in a landscape of having to repeat (Omnidawn, PEN USA best poetry book), Eyetrouble, and Why/Why Not (on Hamlet, University of CA Press). Her work has been included in the anthologies *Lyric Postmodernisms, American Hybrid, Not for Mothers Only,* and most recently *North American Women Poets in the 21st Century,* Wesleyan University Press 2020). She worked as editor for Littoral Books and *The New Review of Literature,* and is the emeritus Irma and Jay Price Professor of English at Occidental College in Los Angeles where she taught Renaissance Literature and creative writing.

The Place One Is
Martha Ronk

Cover photograph by Marth Ronk, color modified by Courtney Gregg

Cover typefaces: Helvetica and Garamond Premier Pro
Interior typeface: Garamond Premier Pro

Cover design by Courtney Gregg. Interior design by Ken Keegan

Printed in the United States
by Books International, Dulles, Virginia
On 55# Glatfelter B19 Antique 360 ppi
Acid Free Archival Quality Recycled Paper

Publication of this book was made possible in part by gifts from
Katherine & John Gravendyk in honor of Hillary Gravendyk,
Francesca Bell, Mary Mackey, and The New Place Fund

Omnidawn Publishing
Oakland, California
Staff and Volunteers, Fall 2021

Rusty Morrison & Ken Keegan, senior editors & co-publishers
Laura Joakimson, production editor and poetry & fiction editor
Rob Hendricks, editor for *Omniverse* & fiction, & post-pub marketing,
Sharon Zetter, poetry editor & book designer
Liza Flum, poetry editor
Matthew Bowie, poetry editor
Anthony Cody, poetry editor
Jason Bayani, poetry editor
Gail Aronson, fiction editor
Jennifer Metsker, marketing assistant